99 Juice and Meal Recipes to Enhance Your Breast Milk Production:

Use the Best Ingredients Available to Increase Your Milk Production

By

Joe Correa CSN

COPYRIGHT

© 2019 Live Stronger Faster Inc.

All rights reserved

Reproduction or translation of any part of this work beyond that permitted by section 107 or 108 of the 1976 United States Copyright Act without the permission of the copyright owner is unlawful.

This publication is designed to provide accurate and authoritative information in regard to the subject matter covered. It is sold with the understanding that neither the author nor the publisher is engaged in rendering medical advice. If medical advice or assistance is needed, consult with a doctor. This book is considered a guide and should not be used in any way detrimental to your health. Consult with a physician before starting this nutritional plan to make sure it's right for you.

ACKNOWLEDGEMENTS

This book is dedicated to my friends and family that have had mild or serious illnesses so that you may find a solution and make the necessary changes in your life.

99 Juice and Meal Recipes to Enhance Your Breast Milk Production:

Use the Best Ingredients Available to Increase Your Milk Production

By

Joe Correa CSN

CONTENTS

Copyright

Acknowledgements

About The Author

Introduction

Commitment

99 Juice and Meal Recipes to Enhance Your Breast Milk Production: Use the Best Ingredients Available to Increase Your Milk Production

Additional Titles from This Author

ABOUT THE AUTHOR

After years of Research, I honestly believe in the positive effects that proper nutrition can have over the body and mind. My knowledge and experience has helped me live healthier throughout the years and which I have shared with family and friends. The more you know about eating and drinking healthier, the sooner you will want to change your life and eating habits.

Nutrition is a key part in the process of being healthy and living longer so get started today. The first step is the most important and the most significant.

INTRODUCTION

99 Juice and Meal Recipes to Enhance Your Breast Milk Production: Use the Best Ingredients Available to Increase Your Milk Production

By Joe Correa CSN

Although most new mothers are a bit skeptical when it comes to changing their nutrition habits, it is extremely important to remember that only a proper and well-balanced diet can provide you and your baby with all the nutrients you need for good health.

In order to achieve this, you must make sure you're eating the right amount and the right types of foods to get the most out of your milk. The best way to do this, without having to spend a lot of time planning and preparing the food, is through juices. Healthy juice recipes are often based on fresh fruits and vegetables your body desperately needs in this particular period of time. When combined with key ingredients, juices truly have the ability to protect your body from toxins accumulated over the years, to improve your overall health, to boost up your immune system, and even to increase your breastmilk production through the nutrients they contain. Furthermore, they take less than 5 minutes to prepare which everyone, especially a new mother, knows how to appreciate.

Having this in mind, I have created these amazingly delicious recipes that will provide all the necessary nutrients you and your child need. I truly hope this book will make some positive changes in your life and give you some new and exciting meal ideas for every day of this wonderful journey you're about to take. I wanted to keep these recipes as simple as possible because I know how important every second with your precious one is.

COMMITMENT

In order to improve my condition, I *(your name)*, commit to eating more of these foods on a daily basis and to exercise at least 30 minutes daily:

- Berries (especially blueberries), peaches, cherries, apples, apricots, oranges, lemon juice, grapefruit, tangerines, mandarins, pears, etc.
- Broccoli, spinach, collard greens, sweet potatoes, avocado, artichoke, baby corn, carrots, celery, cauliflower, onions, etc.
- Whole grains, steel-cut oats, oatmeal, quinoa, barley, etc.
- Black beans, red bean beans, garbanzo beans, lentils, etc.
- Nuts and seeds including: walnuts, cashews, flaxseeds, sesame seeds, etc.
- Fish
- 8 – 10 glasses of water

Sign here

X_____

99 JUICE AND MEAL RECIPES TO ENHANCE YOUR BREAST MILK PRODUCTION: USE THE BEST INGREDIENTS AVAILABLE TO INCREASE YOUR MILK PRODUCTION

JUICE RECIPES

1. Blueberry Lime Juice

Ingredients:

1 cup blueberries

1 whole lime, peeled

1 cup pomegranate seeds

1 small Red Delicious apple, cored

¼ tsp ginger, ground

2 oz water

Preparation:

Place the blueberries in a colander. Rinse well under cold running water and drain. Set aside.

Peel the lime and cut lengthwise in half. Set aside.

Cut the top of the pomegranate fruit using a sharp paring knife. Slice down to each of the white membranes inside of the fruit. Pop the seeds into a measuring cup and set aside.

Wash the apple and cut lengthwise in half. Remove the core and cut into bite-sized pieces and set aside.

Now, combine blueberries, lime, pomegranate seeds, and apple in a juicer and process until juiced. Transfer to a serving glass and stir in the ginger and water.

Refrigerate for 10 minutes before serving.

Enjoy!

Nutritional information per serving: Kcal: 206, Protein: 3.3g, Carbs: 61.1g, Fats: 1.8g

2. Pineapple Grapefruit Juice

Ingredients:

1 cup pineapple, chunked

1 whole grapefruit, peeled and wedged

1 whole lemon, peeled

1 cup black grapes

¼ tsp cinnamon, ground

Preparation:

Using a sharp paring knife, cut the top of the pineapple. Gently remove all hard skin and cut into chunks. Fill the measuring cup and reserve the in the refrigerator.

Peel the grapefruit and divide into wedges. Cut each wedge in half and set aside.

Peel the lemon and cut lengthwise in half. Set aside.

Rinse the grapes thoroughly under running water. Remove the stems and fill the measuring cup. Set aside.

Now, combine pineapple, grapefruit, lemon, and grapes in a juicer and process until juiced. Transfer to a serving glass and stir in the cinnamon.

Add some crushed ice and serve immediately.

Nutritional information per serving: Kcal: 230, Protein: 4g, Carbs: 69.1g, Fats: 1.1g

3. Banana Watermelon Juice

Ingredients:

1 large banana, sliced

1 large watermelon wedge

1 cup strawberries, chopped

2 whole plums, pitted

Preparation:

Peel the banana and cut into thin slices. Set aside.

Cut the watermelon in half. Cut one large wedge and wrap the rest in a plastic foil and refrigerate. Peel the slice and cut into small cubes. Remove the pits and fill the measuring cup. Set aside.

Wash the strawberries and remove the stems. Cut into small pieces and fill the measuring cup. Reserve the rest for in the refrigerator.

Wash the plums and cut into halves. Remove the pits and cut into small pieces. Set aside.

Now, combine banana, watermelon, strawberries, and plums in a juicer and process until juiced. Transfer to a serving glass and add some ice.

Serve immediately.

Nutritional information per serving: Kcal: 273, Protein: 5.1g, Carbs: 78.8g, Fats: 1.6g

4. Peach Plum Juice

Ingredients:

1 large peach, chopped

1 whole plum, chopped

1 cup mango, chopped

1 small Granny Smith's apple, cored

1 oz coconut water

Preparation:

Wash the peach and cut lengthwise in half. Remove the pit and cut into small pieces. Set aside.

Wash the plum and cut in half. Remove the pit and chop into small pieces. Set aside.

Peel the mango and cut into small cubes. Fill the measuring cup and reserve the rest for later.

Wash the apple cut lengthwise in half. Remove the core and chop into small pieces. Set aside.

Now, combine peach, plum, mango, and apple in a juicer and process until juiced. Transfer to a serving glass and stir in the coconut water.

Add some ice and serve immediately.

Nutritional information per serving: Kcal: 252, Protein: 3.8g, Carbs: 71.1g, Fats: 1.6g

5. Blueberry Zucchini Juice

Ingredients:

1 cup blueberries

1 medium-sized zucchini, sliced

2 cups raspberries

1 small ginger knob, peeled

1 oz coconut water

Preparation:

Combine blueberries and raspberries in a large colander. Rinse well under running water. Drain and set aside.

Wash the zucchini and cut into thin slices. Set aside.

Peel the ginger knob and cut into small pieces. Set aside.

Now, combine blueberries, zucchini, raspberries, and ginger in a juicer and process until juiced. Transfer to a serving glass and stir in the coconut water.

Add crushed ice or refrigerate for 15 minutes before serving.

Enjoy!

Nutritional information per serving: Kcal: 164, Protein: 6.5g, Carbs: 58g, Fats: 2.7g

6. Green Melon Raspberry Juice

Ingredients:

1 honeydew melon wedge

1 cup raspberries

1 cup baby spinach, chopped

1 small Granny Smith's apple, cored

¼ tsp ginger, ground

Preparation:

Cut melon lengthwise in half. Scoop out the seeds and then wash the melon. Cut one wedge and peel it. Cut into bite-sized pieces and set aside. Reserve the rest in the refrigerator.

Place the raspberries in a colander and rinse well under cold running water. Drain and set aside.

Wash the spinach thoroughly under cold running water. Drain and chop into small pieces. Set aside.

Wash the apple and cut lengthwise in half. Remove the core and cut into bite-sized pieces. Set aside.

Now, combine melon, raspberries, spinach, and apple in a

juicer and process until juiced. Transfer to a serving glass and stir in the ginger. Add some ice before serving.

Enjoy!

Nutritional information per serving: Kcal: 142, Protein: 4.5g, Carbs: 46.1g, Fats: 1.4g

7. Strawberry Pear Juice

Ingredients:

1 large pear, chopped

1 cup blackberries

1 cup strawberries, chopped

1 small Granny Smith's apple, cored

¼ tsp cinnamon, ground

1 oz water

Preparation:

Wash the pear and cut in half. Remove the core and cut into small pieces. Set aside.

Wash the blackberries using a colander. Drain and set aside.

Wash the strawberries and remove the stems. Cut into small pieces and fill the measuring cup. Reserve the rest in the refrigerator.

Wash the apple and cut lengthwise in half. Remove the core and chop into bite-sized pieces. Set aside.

Now, combine pear, blackberries, strawberries, and apple

in a juicer and process until well juiced. Transfer to a serving glass and stir in the cinnamon.

Refrigerate for 10 minutes before serving.

Enjoy!

Nutritional information per serving: Kcal: 246, Protein: 4.2g, Carbs: 82.1g, Fats: 1.7g

8. Banana Lime Juice

Ingredients:

1 large banana, chopped

1 whole lime, peeled

1 cup watermelon, chopped

1 cup fresh mint, torn

1 small Granny Smith's apple, cored

¼ tsp cinnamon, ground

Preparation:

Peel the banana and cut into small chunks. Set aside.

Peel the lime and cut lengthwise in half. Set aside.

Cut the watermelon in half. Cut one large wedge and wrap the rest in a plastic foil and refrigerate. Peel the slice and cut into small cubes. Remove the pits and fill the measuring cup. Set aside.

Wash the mint thoroughly under cold running water. Drain and torn into small pieces. Set aside.

Wash the apple and cut lengthwise in half. Remove the core and chop into bite-sized pieces. Set aside.

Now, combine banana, lime, watermelon, mint, and apple in a juicer and process until juiced. Transfer to a serving glass and stir in the cinnamon.

Add some crushed ice and serve immediately.

Nutritional information per serving: Kcal: 239, Protein: 4.2g, Carbs: 69.5g, Fats: 1.2g

9. Strawberry Celery Juice

Ingredients:

1 cup strawberries, chopped

1 cup celery, chopped

1 cup apricots, chopped

1 small Golden Delicious apple, cored

¼ tsp cinnamon, ground

Preparation:

Wash the strawberries and remove the stems. Cut into small pieces and fill the measuring cup. Reserve the rest for later.

Wash the celery and chop into small pieces. Set aside.

Wash the apricots and cut in half. Remove the pits and chop into small pieces. Fill the measuring cup and reserve the rest for later. Set aside.

Wash the apple and cut lengthwise in half. Remove the core and cut into small pieces. Set aside.

Now, combine strawberries, celery, apricots, and apple in a juicer and process until juiced. Transfer to a serving glass and stir in the cinnamon.

Add some ice and serve immediately.

Nutritional information per serving: Kcal: 170, Protein: 4.3g, Carbs: 49.9g, Fats: 1.4g

10. Peach Banana Juice

Ingredients:

1 medium-sized peach, chopped

1 large banana, chunked

1 cup mango, chunked

1 large orange, peeled

¼ tsp cinnamon, ground

Preparation:

Wash the peach and cut lengthwise in half. Remove the pit and cut into small pieces. Set aside.

Peel the banana and cut into small chunks. Set aside.

Peel the mango and cut into small chunks. Fill the measuring cup and reserve the rest for later. Set aside.

Peel the orange and divide into wedges. Cut each wedge in half and set aside.

Now, combine peach, banana, mango, and orange in a juicer. Process until well juiced. Transfer to a serving glass and stir in the cinnamon.

Add some crushed ice and serve immediately.

Enjoy!

Nutritional information per serving: Kcal: 313, Protein: 5.9g, Carbs: 91.7g, Fats: 1.6g

11. Plum Cantaloupe Juice

Ingredients:

1 whole plum, chopped

1 cup cantaloupe, chopped

1 large orange, peeled

1 cup fresh mint, torn

¼ tsp turmeric, ground

¼ tsp ginger, ground

Preparation:

Wash the plum and cut in half. Remove the pit and chop into small pieces. Set aside.

Cut the cantaloupe in half. Scoop out the seeds and flesh. Cut and peel one large wedge. Chop into chunks and fill the measuring cup. Reserve the rest of the cantaloupe in a refrigerator.

Peel the orange and divide into wedges. Cut each wedge in half and set aside.

Wash the mint thoroughly under cold running water. Torn into small pieces and set aside.

Now, combine plum, cantaloupe, orange, and mint in a juicer and process until juiced. Transfer to a serving glass and stir in the turmeric and ginger.

Add some ice and serve immediately.

Enjoy!

Nutritional information per serving: Kcal: 151, Protein: 4.4g, Carbs: 45.6g, Fats: 0.9g

12. Avocado Peach Juice

Ingredients:

1 cup avocado, cubed

1 large peach, chopped

1 cup strawberries, chopped

1 large Golden Delicious apple, cored

¼ tsp cinnamon, ground

¼ tsp ginger, ground

2 tsp coconut water

Preparation:

Peel the avocado and cut in half. Remove the pit and cut into small cubes. Fill the measuring cup and reserve the rest for later.

Wash the peach and cut lengthwise in half. Remove the pit and cut into bite-sized pieces. Set aside.

Wash the strawberries and remove the stems. Cut into bite-sized pieces and fill the measuring cup. Reserve the rest for later.

Wash the apple and cut in half. Remove the core and chop

into small pieces. Set aside.

Now, combine avocado, peach, strawberries, and apple in a juicer and process until juiced. Transfer to a serving glass and stir in the cinnamon, ginger, and coconut water.

Refrigerate for 10 minutes before serving.

Nutritional information per serving: Kcal: 386, Protein: 6.5g, Carbs: 68.6g, Fats: 23.2g

13. Cranberry Lemon Juice

Ingredients:

1 cup cranberries

1 whole lemon, peeled

1 large pear, chopped

1 cup watermelon, chunked

¼ tsp cinnamon, ground

1 oz water

Preparation:

Place the cranberries in a colander and rinse under cold running water. Drain and set aside.

Peel the lemon and cut lengthwise in half. Set aside.

Wash the pear and cut in half. Remove the core and cut into small pieces. Set aside.

Cut the watermelon in half. Cut one large wedge and wrap the rest in a plastic foil and refrigerate. Peel the slice and cut into small cubes. Remove the pits and fill the measuring cup. Set aside.

Now, combine cranberries, lemon, pear, and watermelon

in a juicer and process until well juiced. Transfer to a serving glass and stir in the cinnamon and water.

Refrigerate for 5 minutes before serving.

Nutritional information per serving: Kcal: 186, Protein: 2.8g, Carbs: 64.1g, Fats: 0.8g

14. Orange Grape Juice

Ingredients:

1 large orange, peeled

1 cup black grapes

1 cup beets, trimmed and sliced

1 whole apricot, pitted

1 tbsp coconut water

Preparation:

Peel the orange and divide into wedges. Cut each wedge in half and set aside.

Rinse the grapes and remove the stems. Set aside.

Wash the beets and trim off the green parts. Cut into thin slices and fill the measuring cup. Reserve the rest for later.

Wash the apricot and cut lengthwise in half. Remove the pit and cut into small pieces. Set aside.

Now, combine orange, grapes, beets, and apricots in a juicer and process until well juiced. Transfer to a serving glass and stir in the coconut water.

Add some ice and serve immediately.

Nutritional information per serving: Kcal: 184, Protein: 4.9g, Carbs: 54.3g, Fats: 0.9g

15. Mango Grapefruit Juice

Ingredients:

1 cup mango, chunked

1 whole grapefruit, peeled and wedged

2 whole lemons, peeled

1 small Red Delicious apple, cored

¼ tsp ginger, ground

Preparation:

Peel the mango and cut into chunks. Fill the measuring cup and reserve the rest for later. Set aside.

Peel the grapefruit and divide into wedges. Cut each wedge in half and set aside.

Peel the lemons and cut each lengthwise in half. Set aside.

Wash the apple and cut lengthwise in half. Remove the core and cut into bite-sized pieces. Set aside.

Now, combine lemon, mango, grapefruit, and apple in a juicer and process until juiced. Transfer to a serving glass and stir in the ginger.

Add few ice cubes and serve immediately.

Enjoy!

Nutritional information per serving: Kcal: 65, Protein: 4.5g, Carbs: 16.8g, Fats: 0.8g

16. Blackberry Mint Juice

Ingredients:

1 cup blackberries

1 cup fresh mint, chopped

1 cup pineapple, chunked

1 whole lime, peeled

2 oz coconut water

Preparation:

Place the blackberries in a large colander. Rinse thoroughly under cold running water. Drain and set aside.

Wash the mint and drain. Chop into small pieces and set aside.

Using a sharp paring knife, cut the top of the pineapple. Gently remove all hard skin and slice it into thin slices. Fill the measuring cup and reserve the rest for later.

Peel the lime and cut lengthwise in half. Set aside.

Now, combine blackberries, mint, pineapple, and lime in a juicer. Process until well juiced and transfer to a serving glass.

Stir in the coconut water and add few ice cubes before serving.

Enjoy!

Nutritional information per serving: Kcal: 125, Protein: 4g, Carbs: 42.9g, Fats: 1.2g

17. Sour Banana Apple Juice

Ingredients:

1 large banana, chopped

1 small Granny Smith's apple, cored

1 cup pomegranate seeds

1 cup raspberries

¼ tsp ginger, ground

Preparation:

Peel the banana and cut into small pieces. Set aside.

Wash the apple and cut lengthwise in half. Remove the core and cut into bite-sized pieces. Set aside.

Cut the top of the pomegranate fruit using a sharp paring knife. Slice down to each of the white membranes inside of the fruit. Pop the seeds into a measuring cup and set aside.

Rinse the raspberries under cold running water using a colander. Drain and set aside.

Now, combine pomegranate seeds, banana, apple, and raspberries in a juicer and process until juiced. Transfer to a serving glass and stir in the ginger.

Add some ice and serve immediately.

Nutritional information per serving: Kcal: 265, Protein: 5.1g, Carbs: 81.6g, Fats: 2.5g

18. Orange Papaya Juice

Ingredients:

1 large orange, peeled

1 cup papaya, chopped

1 cup cucumber, sliced

1 whole grapefruit, peeled

¼ tsp cinnamon, ground

2 tbsp coconut water

Preparation:

Peel the orange and grapefruit. Divide into wedges. Cut each wedge in half and set aside.

Peel the papaya and cut into small chunks. Fill the measuring cup and reserve the rest in the refrigerator.

Wash the cucumber and cut into thin slices. Fill the measuring cup and reserve the rest for later.

Now, combine orange, papaya, cucumber, and grapefruit in a juicer and process until well juiced.

Transfer to a serving glass and stir in the cinnamon and coconut water.

Refrigerate for 5 minutes before serving.

Nutritional information per serving: Kcal: 214, Protein: 4.6g, Carbs: 65.4g, Fats: 1g

19. Blackberry Blueberry Juice

Ingredients:

¼ cup blackberries

1 cup blueberries

2 large apples, cored and sliced

¼ tsp mint extract

½ cup water

Preparation:

Combine blackberries and blueberries in a colander and wash under cold running water. Drain and set aside.

Wash the apples and remove the core. Cut into bite-sized pieces and set aside.

Now, combine blackberries, blueberries, and apples in a juicer and process until juiced. Transfer to serving glasses and stir in the mint extract and water.

Add few ice cubes before serving.

Enjoy!

Nutritional information per serving: Kcal: 368, Protein: 2.5g, Carbs: 94g, Fats: 1.5g

20. Kale Strawberry Juice

Ingredients:

1 cup fresh kale, torn

1 cup strawberries, fresh

½ tsp ginger, ground

1 whole lemon, peeled

Preparation:

Rinse the kale thoroughly under running water. Torn with your hands and set aside.

Wash the strawberries under cold running water. Drain and set aside.

Peel the lemon and cut lengthwise in half. Set aside.

Combine kale, strawberries, and lemon in a juicer and process until juiced.

Transfer to serving glasses add some ice cubes before serving.

Enjoy!

Nutritional information per serving: Kcal: 120, Protein: 5.9g, Carbs: 38.6g, Fats: 1.8g

21. Grapefruit Peppermint Juice

Ingredients:

1 large grapefruit, peeled

1 tsp peppermint extract

3 large cucumbers, peeled

1 oz coconut water

Preparation:

Peel the grapefruit and cut into bite-sized pieces. set aside.

Wash the cucumbers and cut into thick slices. Set aside.

Now, combine grapefruit and cucumber in a juicer and process until juiced. Transfer to serving glasses and stir in the coconut water, coconut sugar and peppermint extract.

Add some ice cubes and serve immediately.

Nutritional information per serving: Kcal: 204, Protein: 7.7g, Carbs: 59g, Fats: 1.3g

22. Honey Blueberry Juice

Ingredients:

1 tsp honey

1 cup blueberries

1 large banana, peeled

1 cup blackberries

½ tsp cinnamon

Preparation:

Combine blueberries and blackberries in a colander and wash under cold running water. Drain and set aside.

Peel the banana and chop into chunks. Set aside.

Now, combine banana, blueberries, and blackberries in a juicer and process until juiced.

Transfer to serving glasses and stir in the honey and cinnamon.

Add some ice and serve immediately.

Enjoy!

Nutritional information per serving: Kcal: 229, Protein: 4.5g, Carbs: 76.3g, Fats: 1.6g

23. Blueberry Coconut Juice

Ingredients:

1 cup blueberries

½ cup coconut water, unsweetened

2 cups raspberries

½ tsp pure vanilla extract, sugar-free

¼ tsp cinnamon, ground

Preparation:

Wash the raspberries and blueberries under cold running water. Drain well. Transfer all to a juicer and process until juiced.

Transfer to serving glasses and stir in the coconut water, vanilla extract, and cinnamon.

Add few ice cubes and serve immediately.

Enjoy!

Nutritional information per serving: Kcal: 136, Protein: 4.4g, Carbs: 51.7g, Fats: 2.4g

24. Coconut Strawberry Juice

Ingredients:

½ cup coconut water, unsweetened

2 cups strawberries, chopped

1 cup blueberries

½ large red orange

Preparation:

Combine strawberries and blueberries in a colander and wash under cold running water. Set aside.

Peel the orange and divide into wedges. Use about half of the wedges and reserve the rest for some other juice.

Combine strawberries, blueberries, and orange in a juicer. Transfer to serving glasses and stir in the coconut water.

Add some ice or refrigerate before serving.

Nutritional information per serving: Kcal: 246, Protein: 4.7g, Carbs: 74.2g, Fats: 1.7g

25. Lemon Broccoli Juice

Ingredients:

2 large lemons, peeled

1 cup broccoli, chopped

½ cup coconut water, unsweetened

1 cup spinach, torn

1 medium-sized orange

1 tbsp of honey, raw

Preparation:

Peel the lemons and cut lengthwise in half. Set aside.

Wash the broccoli and trim off the outer leaves. Set aside.

Wash the spinach thoroughly and torn with hands. Set aside.

Peel the orange and divide into wedges. Set aside.

Now, combine broccoli, lemons, spinach, and orange in a juicer and process until juiced. Transfer to serving glasses and stir in the honey and garnish with mint leaves.

Add some ice and serve.

Nutritional information per serving: Kcal: 171, Protein: 14.8g, Carbs: 54.5g, Fats: 2.17g

26. Carrot Apple Juice

Ingredients:

2 large carrots, sliced

1 small Granny Smith's apple, cored and chopped

1 cup fresh blueberries

2 cups Romaine lettuce, torn

Preparation:

Wash the carrots and cut into thick slices. Set aside.

Wash the apple and remove the core. Cut into bite-sized pieces and set aside. Wash the blueberries under cold running water. Set aside aside. Wash the lettuce thoroughly and torn with hands. Set aside.

Now, process carrots, apple, blueberries, and lettuce in a juicer. Transfer to serving glasses and add few ice cubes. Serve immediately.

Nutritional information per serving: Kcal: 228, Protein: 6.14g, Carbs: 66.8g, Fats: 1.95g

27. Carrot Broccoli Juice

Ingredients:

1 cup carrots, sliced

1 cup broccoli, chopped

1 cup Brussels sprouts, chopped

1 cup turnip greens, chopped

4 large oranges, peeled

1 tbsp honey

¼ cup pure coconut water

Preparation:

Wash the carrots and cut into thin slices. Set aside.

Wash the broccoli and cut into small pieces. Set aside.

Wash the Brussels sprouts and trim off the outer layers. Cut in half and set aside.

Rinse the turnip greens thoroughly and torn with hands. Set aside.

Peel the oranges and divide into wedges. Set aside.

Now, combine broccoli, Brussels sprouts, carrots, turnip

greens, and oranges in a juicer and process until juiced. Transfer to serving glasses and stir in the honey and coconut water.

Add some ice cubes before serving or refrigerate for 5 minutes.

Enjoy!

Nutrition information per serving: Kcal: 367, Protein: 14.47g, Carbs: 116g, Fats: 1.9g

28. Leafy Green Juice

Ingredients:

1 cup Swiss chard, chopped

1 cup collard greens, chopped

1 cup red leaf lettuce, chopped

1 cup Romaine lettuce, chopped

1 large orange, peeled

1 large cucumber

1 large lemon, peeled

2 oz water

Preparation:

Combine Swiss chard, collard greens, red leaf lettuce, and Romaine lettuce in a colander. Wash under cold running water and drain. Torn with hands and set aside.

Peel the orange and divide into wedges. Set aside.

Wash the cucumber and cut into thick slices. Set aside.

Peel the lemon and cut lengthwise in half. Set aside.

Now, combine Swiss chard, collard greens, red leaf lettuce,

Romaine lettuce, orange, cucumber, and lemon in a juicer and process until juiced.

Transfer to serving glasses and stir in the water.

Add some ice and serve immediately.

Nutrition information per serving: Kcal: 136, Protein: 7g, Carbs: 43.4g, Fats: 1.2g

29. Beet Pineapple Juice

Ingredients:

1 large beet, trimmed

1 cup pineapple chunks

1 cup purple cabbage, chopped

1 large carrot, sliced

1 cup fresh spinach, torn

1 tbsp liquid honey

Preparation:

Wash the beet and trim off the green parts. Cut into small pieces and set aside.

Cut the top of a pineapple and peel it using a sharp knife. Cut into small chunks and fill the measuring cup. Reserve the rest of the pineapple in a refrigerator.

Wash the purple cabbage and spinach thoroughly torn with hands. Set aside.

Wash the carrot and cut into thick slices. Set aside.

Now, combine beet, pineapple, cabbage, carrot, and spinach in a juicer and process until juiced.

Transfer to serving glasses and stir in the liquid honey. Add few ice cubes and serve immediately.

Enjoy!

Nutrition information per serving: Kcal: 205, Protein: 5g, Carbs: 62.1g, Fats: 0.7g

30. Cherry Banana Juice

Ingredients:

1 cup cherries, pitted

1 large banana, peeled

1 cup blueberries

1 whole lemon, peeled

1 small Granny Smith's apple, cored

¼ tsp cinnamon

Preparation:

Wash the cherries and cut in half. Remove the pits and stems. Set aside.

Peel the banana and cut into small chunks. Set aside.

Rinse the blueberries using a large colander. Drain and set aside.

Peel the lemon and cut lengthwise in half. Set aside.

Wash the apple and cut lengthwise in half. Remove the core and cut into small pieces. Set aside.

Now, combine cherries, banana, blueberries, lemon, and

apple in a juicer and process until juiced. Transfer to a serving glass and stir in the cinnamon.

Add some ice and serve immediately.

Nutritional information per serving: Kcal: 340, Protein: 5.5g, Carbs: 102g, Fats: 1.7g

31. Celery Grapefruit Juice

Ingredients:

1 cup celery, chopped

1 whole grapefruit, peeled

2 large carrots, chunked

1 small Golden Delicious apple, cored and chopped

¼ tsp cinnamon, ground

Preparation:

Wash the celery and cut into small pieces. Fill the measuring cup and reserve the rest in the refrigerator.

Peel the grapefruit and divide into wedges. Cut each wedge in half and set aside.

Wash and peel the carrots. Cut into small chunks and set aside.

Wash the apple and cut lengthwise in half. Remove the core and cut into bite-sized pieces. Set aside.

Now, combine celery, grapefruit, carrots, and apple in a juicer and process until well juiced. Transfer to a serving glass and stir in the cinnamon.

Add some crushed ice and serve immediately.

Enjoy!

Nutritional information per serving: Kcal: 203, Protein: 4.3g, Carbs: 60.6g, Fats: 1.1g

32. Strawberry Apple Juice

Ingredients:

1 cup strawberries, chopped

1 small Granny Smith's apple, cored and chopped

1 whole guava, chunked

1 whole lemon, peeled and halved

¼ tsp ginger, ground

2 oz water

Preparation:

Wash the strawberries and remove the stems. Cut into small pieces and fill the measuring cup. Reserve the rest in the refrigerator. Set aside.

Wash the apple and cut lengthwise in half. Remove the core and cut into bite-sized pieces. Set aside.

Peel the guava and cut in half. Scoop out the seeds and wash it. Cut into small chunks and set aside.

Peel the lemon and cut lengthwise in half. Set aside.

Now, combine strawberries, guava, apple, and lemon in a juicer and process until juiced. Transfer to a serving glass and stir in the ginger and water.

Refrigerate for 10 minutes before serving.

Enjoy!

Nutritional information per serving: Kcal: 136, Protein: 3.6g, Carbs: 43.9g, Fats: 1.3g

33. Blackberry Kiwi Juice

Ingredients:

1 cup blackberries

2 whole kiwis, peeled

1 cup cantaloupe, chopped

1 small green apple, cored

¼ tsp ginger, ground

Preparation:

Place the blackberries in a colander. Rinse well under cold running water and drain. Set aside.

Peel the kiwi and cut in half. Set aside.

Cut the cantaloupe in half. Scrape out the seeds and cut one one large wedge. Peel and chop into small pieces. Wrap the rest in a plastic foil and refrigerate for later.

Wash the apple and cut lengthwise in half. Remove the core and cut into bite-sized pieces. Set aside.

Now, combine blackberries, kiwi, cantaloupe, and apple in a juicer and process until juiced. Transfer to a serving glass and stir in the ginger.

Add few ice cubes and serve immediately.

Nutritional information per serving: Kcal: 181, Protein: 4.7g, Carbs: 56.3g, Fats: 1.6g

34. Kale Cucumber Juice

Ingredients:

2 cups kale, chopped

1 cup cucumber, sliced

2 cups broccoli, chopped

1 whole lime, peeled and halved

1 whole lemon, peeled and halved

1 oz water

Preparation:

Wash the kale thoroughly under cold running water. Drain and chop into small pieces. Set aside.

Wash the cucumber and cut into thin slices. Fill the measuring cup and reserve the rest for later.

Wash the broccoli and trim off the outer leaves. Cut into small pieces and fill the measuring cup. Reserve the rest in the refrigerator.

Peel the lime and lemon. Cut each fruit lengthwise in half and set aside.

Now, combine kale, cucumber, broccoli, lime, and lemon in

a juicer and process until juiced. Transfer to a serving glass and stir in the water.

Sprinkle with some mint for some extra taste, but it's optional.

Refrigerate for 5 minutes before serving.

Enjoy!

Nutritional information per serving: Kcal: 116, Protein: 12.1g, Carbs: 34.8g, Fats: 2.2g

35. Banana Avocado Juice

Ingredients:

1 large banana, sliced

1 cup avocado, chunked

1 cup red leaf lettuce, shredded

½ cup strawberries, chopped

1 small Red Delicious apple, cored

¼ tsp cinnamon, ground

Preparation:

Peel the banana and chop into small pieces. Set aside.

Peel the avocado and cut lengthwise in half. Remove the pit and chop into small pieces. Set aside.

Wash the lettuce thoroughly under cold running water. Drain and chop into small pieces. Set aside.

Wash the strawberries and remove the stems. Cut into bite-sized pieces and fill the measuring cup. Set aside.

Now, combine avocado, lettuce, banana, and strawberries in a juicer and process until juiced. Transfer to a serving glass and stir in the cinnamon.

Add some ice and serve immediately.

Enjoy!

Nutritional information per serving: Kcal: 405, Protein: 5.7g, Carbs: 72.2g, Fats: 23.1g

36. Plum Gala Juice

Ingredients:

2 whole plums, pitted and chopped

1 Gala apple, cored

1 cup cherries, pitted

1 cup strawberries, chopped

1 tbsp coconut water

¼ tsp ginger, ground

Preparation:

Wash the cherries thoroughly using a large colander. Drain and cut each in half. Remove the pits and cut into small pieces. Set aside.

Wash the plums and cut in half. Remove the pits and cut into small bite-sized pieces. Set aside.

Wash the apple and cut lengthwise in half. Remove the core and cut into small pieces. Set aside.

Wash the strawberries and remove the stems. Cut into small pieces and fill the measuring cup. Reserve the rest for later. Set aside.

Now, combine plums, apple, cherries, and strawberries in a juicer and process until juiced. Transfer to a serving glass and stir in the coconut water and ginger.

Add some crushed ice and serve immediately.

Nutritional information per serving: Kcal: 236, Protein: 4.2g, Carbs: 70.3g, Fats: 1.3g

37. Carrot Radish Juice

Ingredients:

2 large carrots, sliced

1 large radish, chopped

1 cup cauliflower, chopped

1 cup turnip greens, torn

¼ tsp ginger, ground

2 oz water

Preparation:

Wash and peel the carrots. Cut into thin slices and set aside.

Wash the radish and chop into small pieces. Set aside.

Trim off the outer leaves of the cauliflower. Wash it and chop into small pieces. Fill the measuring cup and reserve the rest for later.

Wash the turnip greens thoroughly under cold running water. Drain and torn into small pieces. Set aside.

Now, combine carrots, radish, cauliflower, and turnip greens in a juicer and process until juiced. Transfer to a serving glass and stir in the ginger and water.

Add some ice and serve immediately.

Nutritional information per serving: Kcal: 75, Protein: 4.3g, Carbs: 23.3g, Fats: 0.8g

38. Spinach Watercress Juice

Ingredients:

2 cups spinach, torn

1 cup watercress, torn

1 cup kale, torn

1 cup Swiss chard, torn

¼ tsp ginger, ground

1 oz water

Preparation:

Combine, spinach, watercress, kale, and Swiss chard in a large colander. Rinse thoroughly under cold running water. Slightly drain and torn into small pieces.

Now, combine spinach, watercress, kale, and Swiss chard in a juicer and process until juiced. Transfer to a serving glass and stir in the ginger and water.

Refrigerate for 10 minutes before serving.

Enjoy!

Nutritional information per serving: Kcal: 87, Protein: 16.3g, Carbs: 22.9g, Fats: 2.4g

39. Avocado Kale Juice

Ingredients:

1 cup avocado, cubed

1 cup fresh kale, torn

2 cups Iceberg lettuce, torn

1 whole kiwi, peeled

1 whole cucumber, sliced

Preparation:

Peel the avocado and cut lengthwise in half. Remove the pit and cut into small cubes. Fill the measuring cup and reserve the rest for later.

Combine kale and lettuce in a large colander. Wash thoroughly under cold running water and torn into small pieces. Set aside.

Peel the kiwi and cut lengthwise in half. Set aside.

Wash the cucumber and cut into thin slices. Fill the measuring cup and reserve the rest for later.

Now, combine avocado, kale, lettuce, kiwi, and cucumber in a juicer and process until juiced. Transfer to a serving glass and add some ice before serving.

Enjoy!

Nutritional information per serving: Kcal: 304, Protein: 9.8g, Carbs: 42.8g, Fats: 23.6g

40. Apple Strawberry Juice

Ingredients:

1 large Golden Delicious apple, cored and chopped

1 cup fresh strawberries, chopped

1 cup beets, sliced

1 large lime, peeled

1 small ginger root knob

1 tbsp liquid honey

2 oz water

Preparation:

Wash the apple and remove the core. Cut into bite-sized pieces. Set aside.

Place the strawberries in a colander and wash under cold running water. Drain and cut in half. Set aside.

Wash the beets and trim off the green parts. Cut into small pieces and fill the measuring cup. Reserve the beet greens for some other juice. Set aside.

Peel the lime and cut lengthwise in half. Set aside.

Peel the ginger root knob and set aside.

Now, combine apple, strawberries, beets, and ginger in a juicer and process until juiced. Transfer to serving glasses and stir in honey and water.

Add some ice and serve immediately.

Nutrition information per serving: Kcal: 277, Protein: 4.2g, Carbs: 82.4g, Fats: 1.3g

41. Squash Banana Juice

Ingredients:

1 cup butternut squash, chunked

1 medium-sized banana, peeled

½ cup coconut water

1 cup raspberries, fresh

1 tsp honey, raw

Preparation:

Peel the butternut squash and remove the seeds using a spoon. Cut into small cubes and reserve the rest of the squash for some other recipe. Wrap in a plastic foil and refrigerate.

Peel the banana and cut into chunks. Set aside.

Rinse the raspberries under cold running water. Drain and set aside.

Now, combine butternut squash, banana, and raspberries in a juicer. Transfer to serving glasses and stir in the coconut water and honey.

Add some ice and serve immediately.

Enjoy!

Nutritional information per serving: Kcal: 197, Protein: 4.7g, Carbs: 68g, Fats: 1.3g

42. Cranberry Kiwi Juice

Ingredients:

1 cup cranberries

3 large kiwis, peeled

1 cup kale, torn

1 tbsp coconut water

Preparation:

Wash the cranberries under cold running water. Drain and set aside.

Peel the kiwis and cut lengthwise in half. Set aside.

Wash the kale thoroughly and torn with hands. Set aside.

Now, combine cranberries, kiwis, and kale in a juicer. Transfer to serving glasses and stir in the coconut water.

Add some ice and serve!

Nutritional information per serving: Kcal: 153, Protein: 5.6g, Carbs: 48.4g, Fats: 1.8g

43. Cucumber Apple Juice

Ingredients:

4 cups cucumber, sliced

3 large Granny Smith apples, cored

1 large lemon, peeled

¼ cup water

1 tbsp liquid honey

Preparation:

Wash the cucumber and cut into thick slices. Set aside. Wash the apples and remove the core. Cut into bite-sized pieces and set aside. Peel the lemon and cut lengthwise in half. Set aside. Now, combine cucumber, apples, and lemon in a juicer and process until juiced. Transfer to serving glasses and stir in the water and liquid honey. Garnish with some fresh mint, but this is optional.

Add few ice cubes before serving and enjoy!

Nutrition information per serving: Kcal: 327, Protein: 4.7g, Carbs: 97g, Fats: 1.5g

44. Kale Mango Juice

Ingredients:

2 cups kale, torn

1 cup mango, chopped

4 whole kiwis, peeled

1 tbsp fresh mint, finely chopped

Preparation:

Rinse the kale thoroughly under running water. Remove the hard stems from the middle and torn with hands into small pieces. Set aside.

Peel the mango and cut into small chunks. Set aside.

Peel the kiwis and cut lengthwise in half. Set aside.

Now, combine kale, mango, and kiwis in a juicer and process until juiced.

Transfer to serving glasses and add few ice cubes. Garnish with fresh mint and serve immediately.

Nutritional information per serving: Kcal: 272, Protein: 10.3g, Carbs: 77g, Fats: 3.3g

45. Watermelon Ginger Juice

Ingredients:

1 cup watermelon, diced

1 small ginger knob

1 cup watercress, chopped

1 whole lime, peeled

1 cup blueberries

Preparation:

Cut the watermelon lengthwise. For one cup, you will need about 1 large wedge. Peel and cut into chunks. Remove the seeds and set aside. Reserve the rest of for some other juices.

Peel the ginger slice and set aside.

Wash the watercress thoroughly and roughly chop it. Set aside.

Peel the lime and cut lengthwise in half. Set aside.

Wash the blueberries under cold running water and set aside.

Now, process, watermelon, ginger, watercress, lime, and

blueberries in a juicer.

Transfer to serving glasses and add some ice.

Serve immediately.

Nutritional information per serving: Kcal: 129, Protein: 3g, Carbs: 37.4g, Fats: 0.8g

46. Artichoke Broccoli Juice

Ingredients:

2 large artichokes, peeled and chopped

1 cup fresh broccoli

1 cup mustard greens, torn

1 cup fresh basil, torn

1 large cucumber

¼ cup spinach, torn

Preparation:

Trim off the outer leaves of artichokes using a sharp knife. Cut into small pieces and set aside.

Wash the broccoli and cut into small pieces. Set aside.

Combine mustard greens, basil, and spinach in a colander. Wash under cold running water and torn with hands. Set aside.

Wash the cucumber and cut into thick slices. Set aside.

Now, process artichokes, broccoli, mustard greens, basil, spinach, and cucumber in a juicer.

Transfer to serving glasses. You can add some salt, but this is optional.

Refrigerate for 5 minutes before serving.

Nutritional information per serving: Kcal: 157, Protein: 18.3g, Carbs: 55.4g, Fats: 1.6g

47. Cantaloupe Mango Juice

Ingredients:

1 cup cantaloupe, peeled and cubed

1 large mango, chunked

1 large cucumber, sliced

2 tbsp fresh mint

Preparation:

Cut the cantaloupe in half. Scoop out the seeds and flesh. Cut two wedges and peel them. Chop into chunks and set aside. Reserve the rest of the cantaloupe in a refrigerator.

Peel the mango and cut into bite-sized pieces. Set aside.

Wash the cucumber and cut into thick slices. Set aside.

Now, process cantaloupe, mango, and cucumber in a juicer.

Transfer to serving glasses and add few ice cubes before serving.

Garnish with mint leaves and enjoy!

Nutrition information per serving: Kcal: 268, Protein: 6.1g, Carbs: 74.4g, Fats: 1.9g

48. Cherry Kiwi Juice

Ingredients:

1 cup cherries, pitted

2 large kiwis, peeled

1 large Granny Smith apple, cored

1 cup pineapple, chunked

Preparation:

Wash the cherries under cold running water. Drain and remove the pits. Set aside.

Peel the kiwis and cut lengthwise in half. Set aside.

Wash the apple and remove the core. Cut into bite-sized pieces and set aside.

Cut the top of a pineapple and peel it using a sharp knife. Cut into small chunks. Reserve the rest of the pineapple in a refrigerator.

Now, combine cherries, kiwis, apple, and pineapple in a juicer and process until juiced.

Transfer to serving glasses and serve immediately.

Nutrition information per serving: Kcal: 287, Protein: 4.2g, Carbs: 84.5g, Fats: 1.2g

49. Carrot Apricot Juice

Ingredients:

1 large carrot, sliced

1 cup apricots, pitted and halved

1 large lemon, peeled

1 Granny Smith's apple, cored and chopped

1 tbsp liquid honey

2 oz water

Preparation:

Wash the carrot and cut into thick slices and set aside.

Wash the apricots and cut in half. Remove the pits and fill the measuring cup. Reserve the rest for some other juice. Set aside.

Peel the lemon and cut lengthwise in half. Set aside.

Wash the apple and remove the core. Cut into bite-sized pieces and set aside.

Now, combine carrot, apricots, lemon, and apple in a juicer and process until juiced.

Transfer to serving glasses and stir in the liquid honey and water.

Refrigerate for 5 minutes before serving.

Nutrition information per serving: Kcal: 243, Protein: 4.2g, Carbs: 69.3g, Fats: 1.3g

50. Gala Grapefruit Juice

Ingredients:

1 medium-sized Gala apple, cored

1 large grapefruit, peeled

1 cup raspberries

1 large carrot

1 small ginger knob

1 oz water

Preparation:

Wash the apple and remove the core. Cut into bite-sized pieces. Set aside.

Peel the grapefruit and divide into wedges. Set aside.

Place the raspberries in a colander and wash under cold running water. Drain and set aside.

Wash the carrot and cut into thick slices. Set aside.

Peel the ginger root and set aside.

Now, process apple, grapefruit, raspberries, carrot, and ginger in a juicer.

Transfer to serving glasses and stir in the water. Add few ice cubes or refrigerate before serving.

Enjoy!

Nutrition information per serving: Kcal: 239, Protein: 4.9g, Carbs: 76.2g, Fats: 1.7g

51. Strawberry Kiwi Juice

Ingredients:

1 cup of fresh strawberries, chopped

2 whole kiwis, peeled

1 large cucumber, sliced

1 small lime, peeled

2 tbsp fresh mint

Preparation:

Wash the strawberries and cut into halves. Set aside.

Peel the kiwis and cut into halves. Set aside.

Wash the cucumber and chop into bite-sized pieces.

Peel the lime and cut into quarters. Set aside.

Wash the mint leaves and soak in water for 5 minutes.

Now, combine strawberries, kiwis, cucumber, lime, and mint in a juicer. Process until nicely juiced.

Transfer to serving glasses and refrigerate for 5 minutes before serving.

Nutritional information per serving: Kcal: 91, Protein: 3.1g, Carbs: 29.9g, Fats: 0.9g

52. Plum Cucumber Juice

Ingredients:

1 large cucumber, sliced

2 cups green grapes

1 cup fresh plums, pitted and chopped

1 cup mustard greens, torn

1 small ginger root slice

Preparation:

Wash the cucumber and cut into thick slices. Set aside.

Rinse the grapes under cold running water. Drain and set aside.

Wash the plums and cut in half. Remove the pits and chop into bite-sized pices- Set aside.

Rinse the mustard greens thoroughly and torn with hands. Set aside.

Peel the ginger root slice and set aside.

Now, process cucumber, grapes, plums, mustard greens, and ginger in a juicer.

Transfer to serving glasses and refrigerate for 5 minutes before serving.

Enjoy!

Nutrition information per serving: Kcal: 339, Protein: 6.9g, Carbs: 56.7g, Fats: 21.9g

53. Asparagus Collard Greens Juice

Ingredients:

1 cup asparagus, trimmed and chopped

1 cup collard greens, torn

1 medium-sized tomato, chopped

1 cup spinach, torn

¼ tsp salt

Preparation:

Wash the asparagus and trim off the woody ends. Cut into small pieces and fill the measuring cup. Set aside.

Combine collard greens and spinach in a large colander. Rinse under cold running water and drain. Torn into small pieces and set aside.

Wash the tomato and place it in a small bowl. Cut into small pieces and reserve the tomato juice while cutting. Set aside.

Now, combine asparagus, collard greens, tomato, and spinach in a juicer and process until juiced. Transfer to a serving glass and stir in the reserve tomato juice and salt. Optionally, sprinkle with some freshly ground rosemary.

Serve immediately.

Nutritional information per serving: Kcal: 66, Protein: 11.2g, Carbs: 19.6g, Fats: 1.5g

MEAL RECIPES

1. Brussel Sprout Risotto

Ingredients:

1 lb lamb, tender cuts

1 cup rice

12 oz brussels sprouts

¼ cup sweet corn

4-5 pieces baby corn

2 tbsp butter, softened

1 tbsp turmeric, ground

1 tsp sea salt

¼ tsp freshly ground black pepper

3 cups lamb's broth

Preparation:

Rinse the meat under cold running water and pat dry with a kitchen paper. Place on a clean working surface and using a sharp knife, cut into bite-sized pieces. Place the meat at the bottom of a large, heavy-bottomed pot. Add three cups of water and cover with a lid. Simmer for 30 minutes, over medium heat.

Remove the meat but reserve the liquid for the rice. Now add rice and season with salt, pepper, and ground turmeric. Cook for another 8 minutes, stirring occasionally. Finally, add meat chops and give it a good stir. Cook for five more minutes.

Meanwhile, melt the butter in a large skillet. Add Brussels sprouts, corn, and baby corn. Cook for about 15 minutes, stirring constantly until the sprouts are nicely browned and lightly charred. Serve with rice and meat. Optionally, add some more pepper or salt to taste.

Nutrition information per serving: Kcal: 491, Protein: 34.8g, Carbs: 61.4g, Fats: 13.4g

2. Chicken Pudding with Artichoke

Ingredients:

1 lb dark and white chicken meat, cooked

2 artichokes

2 tbsp of butter, unsalted

2 tbsp of extra virgin olive oil

1 lemon, juiced

1 handful of fresh parsley leaves

1 tsp of pink Himalayan salt

¼ tsp of freshly ground black pepper

½ tsp of ground chili pepper, for topping

Preparation:

If possible, use organic chicken meat (breast and thighs). Thoroughly rinse the meat and pat dry with a kitchen paper. Using a sharp paring knife, cut the meat into smaller pieces and remove the bones. Rub with olive oil and set aside.

Heat the saute pan over medium-high heat. Turn the heat down slightly to medium and add the meat. Cook for about one minute to get it a little golden one one side. Then flip each piece, cover the pan with a thigh fitting lid and turn the heat to low. Cook for ten minutes without removing the lid. This will poach your meat from the inside out in its own juices. This is why it's important that the lid stays on all the time.

Now turn off the heat and let it sit for another ten minutes. It has to stay covered the whole time. Take the lid off the pan and set aside allowing the meat to cool for a while.

Meanwhile, prepare the artichoke. Cut the lemon into halves and squeeze the juice in a small bowl. Divide the juice in half and set aside.

Using a sharp paring knife, trim off the outer leaves until you reach the yellow and soft ones. Trim off the green outer skin around the artichoke base and stem. Make sure to remove the 'hairs' around the artichoke heart. They are inedible so simply throw them away. Cut artichoke into half-inch pieces. Rub with half of the lemon juice and place in a heavy-bottomed pot. Add enough water to cover and cook until completely fork-tender. Remove from the heat and drain. Chill for a while (to a room temperature). I like to cut each piece into thin strips, but this is optional.

Now combine artichoke with chicken meat in a large bowl. Stir in salt, pepper, and the remaining lemon juice. Melt the butter over medium heat and drizzle over pudding.

Sprinkle with some chili pepper and parsley. Serve.

Nutrition information per serving: Kcal: 486, Protein: 47.4g, Carbs: 11.5g, Fats: 28.4g

3. Chicken Risotto with Soaked Pide

Ingredients:

1 lb chicken meat, dark and white parts

½ cup rice

4 cups chicken broth

1 large pide bread, chopped into bite-sized pieces

1 tsp salt

½ tsp freshly ground black pepper

Sour cream for topping (optionally)

Preparation:

If possible, use organic chicken meat (breast and thighs). Thoroughly rinse the meat and pat dry with a kitchen paper. Using a sharp paring knife, cut the meat into smaller pieces and remove the bones. Rub with salt and place in a deep pot. Add 4 cups of chicken broth and cook for 30 minutes.

When the meat is fork-tender, remove from the pot but keep the liquid. Add rice and cook for 10 minutes, stirring occasionally.

Meanwhile, cut the chicken meat into bite-sized pieces and place in a large bowl. Set aside.

In another bowl, cut pide bread into bite-sized pieces. Add rice and the remaining broth to soak the pide bread. Stir in chicken chops and let it stand for 15 more minutes. Sason with salt and pepper before serving.

Optionally top with sour cream.

Nutrition information per serving: Kcal: 445, Protein: 43.7g, Carbs: 48.1g, Fats: 6.8g

4. Braised Spinach and Leeks

Ingredients:

12 oz fresh spinach

3 large leeks, sliced

2 red onions, sliced

2 garlic cloves, crushed

½ cup goat's cheese

3 tbsp extra virgin olive oil

1 tsp sea salt

Preparation:

Heat up the olive oil over medium-high heat. Add sliced leek, garlic, and onions. Stir-fry for about five minutes, over medium heat. Now add spinach and give it a good stir. Season with sea salt and continue to cook for 3 more minutes, stirring constantly. Remove from the heat and sprinkle with fresh goat's cheese. Serve immediately.

Nutrition information per serving: Kcal: 301, Protein: 9.6g, Carbs: 24.7g, Fats: 20.4g

5. Creamy Cheese Bread with Olive oil

Ingredients:

14 oz whole wheat flour

1 ¼ cup lukewarm water

2 tbsp olive oil

1 tsp baking powder

1 tsp honey

1 tsp salt

2 tbsp dry yeast

<u>For filling:</u>

1 cup Feta cheese

3 tbsp fresh rosemary, finely chopped

3 spring onions, sliced

2 garlic cloves, crushed

½ cup olives

6-7 peppercorns

¼ cup olive oil

Preparation:

Combine all dry ingredients in a large bowl. Gradually add water beating well after each addition. Now add olive oil and stir well. Cover with a clean towel and let it stand for 30 minutes at the room temperature.

Knead 10 to 15 minutes until dough is smooth and elastic. Place in a lightly greased bowl and let it rise for one hour.

Preheat the oven to 375 degrees and bake for 30 minutes. Remove from the oven chill for a while.

Using a sharp paring knife, cut the bread and fill with Feta cheese, finely chopped rosemary, crushed garlic, olives, peppercorns, and olive oil. Bake for 10 more minutes.

Remove from the oven and chill completely. Sprinkle with sliced spring onions and serve.

Nutrition information per serving: Kcal: 349, Protein: 8.1g, Carbs: 34.3g, Fats: 20.7g

6. Mediterranean Scallops

Ingredients:

4 large Mediterranean scallops, cleaned

4 tbsp extra virgin olive oil

1 tsp sea salt

1 tsp garlic powder

1 tbsp freshly squeezed lemon juice

1 tsp dried rosemary

1 cup white wine

Preparation:

Rinse well scallops under cold running water. Place in a heavy-bottomed pot and pour in white wine, rosemary, lemon juice, garlic powder, salt, and olive oil. Add one cup of water and bring it to a boil. Cook until barely tender, 3-4 minutes. Reduce the heat to medium and simmer for ten more minutes.

Remove from the heat and chill for a while. Place each scallop on a serving plate and brush with the remaining liquid.

Serve with wild asparagus salad.

Nutrition information per serving: Kcal: 340, Protein: 20.9g, Total Carb: 9.2g, Dietary Fiber: 0.9g, Sugars: 1.9g, Total Fat: 15.2g, Saturated Fat: 2.3g

7. Wild asparagus salad

Ingredients:

7 oz fresh wild asparagus

3 tbsp extra virgin olive oil

2 garlic cloves, crushed

2 tbsp freshly squeezed lemon juice

½ tsp sea salt

Preparation:

Rinse well the asparagus and cut into one-inch-long pieces. Drain and set aside.

Heat up the olive oil in a large non-stick skillet. Add garlic and stir-fry for three minutes. Now add asparagus and continue to cook for ten more minutes, stirring constantly.

Remove from the heat and season with salt and lemon juice.

8. Spring Vegetable Soup

Ingredients:

1 medium-sized carrot, finely chopped

2 spring onions, finely chopped

1 yellow bell pepper, finely chopped and seeds removed

2 celery stalks, finely chopped

½ cup celery leaves, finely chopped

½ tsp dried thyme

2 tbsp butter

1 tsp vegetable oil

4 cups vegetable broth

1 cup milk

1 tsp salt

¼ tsp black pepper, freshly ground

Preparation:

Heat up the oil in a large, heavy-bottomed pan. Add butter and allow it to melt. Now add finely chopped carrot, spring onions, bell pepper, and celery stalks. Cook for ten minutes, stirring constantly.

Pour in vegetable broth and bring it to a boil. Reduce the heat to medium and add milk, celery leaves, thyme, salt, and pepper.

Cook for 15 minutes stirring occasionally.

Nutrition information per serving: Kcal: 150, Protein: 7.6g, Total Carb: 8.6g, Dietary Fiber: 1.2g, Sugars: 6g, Total Fat: 9.6g, Saturated Fat: 5g

9. Bell Pepper Risotto with Chicken

Ingredients:

12 oz of chicken breasts, boneless, skinless, and cut into bite-sized pieces

1 cup of rice

7 oz of button mushrooms, sliced

1 red bell pepper, halved and seeds removed

1 green bell pepper, halved and seeds removed

1 yellow bell pepper, halved and seeds removed

7 oz of cauliflower florets

5-6 baby corn

½ cup of sweet corn

2 medium-sized carrots, peeled and chopped

2 tbsp of olive oil

1 tbsp of butter

1 tsp of salt

½ tsp of freshly ground black pepper

1 tsp of fresh rosemary, finely chopped

Preparation:

First, you will have to prepare the rice. Place one cup of rice in a deep pot. Add 3 cups of water and a pinch of salt. Bring it to a boil and reduce the heat to medium-low. Cook until the water evaporates, stirring occasionally. Remove from the heat and set aside.

Rinse and clean the vegetables. Pat dry and cut each pepper in half. Remove the seeds and thinly slice, or chop each pepper. Finely chop the carrots because they take a long time to cook, so you want them as smaller as possible. Divide cauliflower into small florets. Remove the stems from button mushrooms and slice them.

Now, grease a large skillet with two tablespoons of oil and add carrots and cauliflower. Cook for 15 minutes. Now, add corn, baby corn, and bell peppers. Continue to cook for 5 minutes, stirring constantly. Finally, add mushrooms, give it a good stir and cook for 3-4 minutes. Remove from the heat and combine with rice. Set aside.

Meanwhile, prepare the chicken. Rinse well the meat under cold running water and pat dry using a kitchen paper. Place on a clean working surface. With a sharp paring knife, gently remove the skin and bones. Chop chicken breasts into bite-sized pieces. Place in a deep pot and cook until fork tender. Drain and combine with rice and vegetables. Serve warm and optionally top with Greek yogurt.

Nutrition information per serving: Kcal: 530, Protein: 30.8g, Carbs: 73g, Dietary Fibers: 8.2g, Sugars: 12g, Fats: 15.5g, Saturated Fats: 4.1g

10. Soft Chicken with Spinach

Ingredients:

2 lbs organic chicken meat, dark and white meat

5 oz fresh spinach, torn

2 cups of chicken broth, homemade

2 tbsp butter, unsalted

2 tbsp olive oil

1 tsp sea salt

Preparation:

If possible, use organic chicken meat (breast and thighs). Thoroughly rinse the meat and pat dry with a kitchen paper. Using a sharp paring knife, cut the meat into smaller pieces.

Rinse well the spinach. Always look for organic vegetables. They can be a bit messier to clean but are definitely worth it. Chop and drain in a colander.

Grease a large heavy-bottomed pot with olive oil. Place the meat in it and pour in two cups of chicken broth. Add salt and cook for about one hour over medium temperature. When the meat is completely fork-tender, remove from the heat and drain in a large colander. You can reserve the liquid for a nice chicken soup.

Melt the butter in a large skillet, over medium-high heat. Add chopped spinach and stir-fry for 3-4 minutes, stirring constantly. Now add ¼ cup of water and continue to cook until the water evaporates.

Serve together and season with some more salt if needed. I like to add some freshly ground turmeric before serving, but this is completely optional.

Nutrition information per serving: Kcal: 484, Protein: 57.8g, Carbs: 7.2g, Fats: 24.7g

11. Chickpea Stew with Onions

Ingredients:

1 lb chickpeas, soaked

3 large purple onions, peeled and sliced

2 large tomatoes, roughly chopped

3 oz parsley, chopped

2 cups vegetable broth

1 tbsp cayenne pepper

3 tbsp butter

2 tbsp olive oil

1 tsp salt

½ tsp freshly ground black pepper

Preparation:

Heat up the oil in a large skillet. Add onions and cook until translucent. Now add soaked chickpeas, chopped tomatoes, chopped parsley, and vegetable broth. Stir in cayenne pepper, salt, and freshly ground black pepper.

Reduce the heat to minimum and simmer for 45 minutes,

stirring occasionally. Serve warm.

Nutrition information per serving: Kcal: 513, Protein: 21.8g, Carbs: 68.3g, Dietary Fibers: 19.4g, Sugars: 16g, Fats: 19.1g, Saturated Fats: 6g

12. Thick Tomato Stew

Ingredients:

2 lbs pork stew meat

1 large eggplant, chopped into bite-sized pieces

4 large tomatoes, peeled and roughly chopped

4 tbsp sunflower oil

2 bay leaves

2 tbsp of tomato paste, homemade

1 tbsp of Cayenne pepper, ground

½ tsp of chili pepper, ground (optional)

½ tsp of salt

Preparation:

Rinse the pork and season with salt and pepper.

Grease the bottom of a large, heavy-bottomed pot with oil. Heat up the oil over medium heat and add pork. Brown the meat on all sides for about 15 minutes. Now add tomatoes and eggplants and continue to cook for five more minutes, stirring constantly.

Reduce the heat to minimum and add two cups of water. Stir in two tablespoons of homemade tomato paste, cayenne pepper, and optionally chili pepper. Add two bay leaves and some more salt to taste. Cover and cook for about 45 minutes, or until pork is completely tender.

Nutrition information per serving: Kcal: 408, Protein: 49.7g, Carbs: 11.1g, Fats: 18.1g

13. Cold Okra Salad

Ingredients:

7 oz fresh okra, whole

7 oz bean sprouts, trimmed

½ cup green peas, pre-cooked

2 medium-sized carrots, sliced into strips

7 oz cherry tomatoes, whole

3.5 oz baby corn, whole

3 garlic cloves, crushed

3 tbsp extra virgin olive oil

¼ cup vegetable broth

½ tsp sea salt

1 tbsp fresh rosemary, finely chopped

Preparation:

Rinse the vegetables and drain in a large colander. Peel and slice carrots into thin strips. Place in a large non-stick skillet and cook for 8-10 minutes, stirring constantly. Remove from the heat and set aside.

Now heat up the olive oil and add garlic and rosemary. Stir-fry until translucent, for about 3-4 minutes. Now add vegetables, vegetable broth, and salt. Cook until the liquid evaporates.

Remove from the heat and serve warm.

Nutrition information per serving: Kcal: 235, Protein: 7.4g, Carbs: 32.3g, Dietary Fibers: 6.3g, Sugars: 7.3g, Fats: 10.2g, Saturated Fats: 1.5g

14. Collard Greens with Shrimps

Ingredients:

1 lb collard greens, chopped

1 lb shrimps, whole

7 oz octopus, chopped into bite-sized pieces

1 large tomato, peeled and finely chopped

3 cups fish stock

4 tbsp extra virgin olive oil

3 garlic cloves

2 tbsp fresh parsley, finely chopped

1 tsp sea salt

Preparation:

Rinse well the greens and drain in a large colander. Place on a clean working surface and chop with a sharp knife. Set aside.

Now place shrimps and octopus in a large, deep pot. Add chopped tomato and fish stock. Cover with a lid and cook for 40 minutes, over medium-high heat, until octopus is fork-tender. Remove from the heat and drain.

Now, grease the bottom of your pot with olive oil and add garlic and parsley. Stir-fry until translucent, stirring constanty.

Finally, add chopped collard greens and simmer for 10 more minutes. Season with salt and give it a good stir. Remove from the heat and serve with shrimps and octopus.

Nutrition information per serving: Kcal: 368, Protein: 40.3g, Carbs: 10.9g, Dietary Fibers: 4g, Sugars: 0g, Fats: 18.9g, Saturated Fats: 3.1g

15. Collard Greens with Veal

Ingredients:

1 lb of veal brisket, cut into half-inch thick pieces

2 lbs of collard greens, torn

¼ cup of rice

2 garlic cloves, crushed

¼ cup of olive oil

2 tsp of sea salt

½ lemon, juiced

Preparation:

Rinse well the meat under the running water. Pat dry using a kitchen paper and sprinkle with salt. Set aside.

Heat up three tablespoons of olive oil in a large pot. Add meat and briefly brown on all sides. Now add about one cup of water and reduce the heat. Simmer until fork tender. Now add rice and one more cup of water. Continue to cook until the liquid evaporates.

Add greens, garlic, and the remaining olive oil. Cover with a lid and simmer for five minutes over minimum temperature.

Serve warm.

Nutrition information per serving: Kcal: 410, Protein: 33.5g, Carbs: 22.2g, Dietary Fibers: 7.7g, Sugars: 0g, Fats: 22.8g, Saturated Fats: 5.3g

16. Fresh Tomato and Celery Soup

Ingredients:

1 lb tomatoes, peeled and roughly chopped

3.5 oz celery root, finely chopped

¼ cup fresh celery leaves, finely chopped

1 tbsp of fresh basil, finely chopped

Salt and pepper to taste

5 tbsp extra virgin olive oil

Preparation:

Preheat the oil in a large non-stick frying pan over a medium-high temperature. Add finely chopped celery root, celery leaves, and fresh basil. Season with salt and pepper and stir-fry for about 10 minutes, until nicely browned.

Add chopped tomatoes and about ¼ cup of water. Reduce the heat to minimum and cook for 15 minutes, stirring constantly, until softened. Now add about 4 cups of water (or vegetable broth) and bring it to a boil. Give it a good stir and remove from the heat.

Top with fresh parsley and serve.

Nutrition information per serving: Kcal: 182, Protein: 1.4g, Carbs: 6.9g, Dietary Fibers: 1.9g, Sugars: 3.5g, Fats: 17.8g, Saturated Fats: 2.6g

17. Creamy Wild Asparagus Soup

Ingredients:

2 lbs fresh wild asparagus, trimmed

2 small onions, peeled and finely chopped

1 cup of heavy cream

4 cups of vegetable broth

2 tbsp of butter

1 tbsp of vegetable oil

½ tsp of salt

½ tsp of dried oregano

½ tsp of cayenne pepper

Preparation:

Rinse and drain asparagus. Cut into about one inch thick pieces. Set aside.

Melt the butter in a large skillet and add oil. Heat up and add onions. Cook until translucent.

Now add trimmed asparagus, oregano, salt, and cayenne pepper. Stir well and continue to cook until asparagus soften.

Add the vegetable broth and mix well to combine. Cook for 15 minutes, stirring occasionally.

Whisk in one cup of heavy cream and serve.

Nutrition information per serving: Kcal: 284, Protein: 11g, Carbs: 14.1g, Dietary Fibers: 5.6g, Sugars: 6.5g, Fats: 22g, Saturated Fats: 11.7g

18. Toasted Pine Nuts Salad

Ingredients:

2 oz of Swiss chard, chopped

1 medium-sized yellow bell pepper, sliced

1 small green apple, cored and chopped

¼ cup of pine nuts, lightly toasted

¼ of fennel bulb, chopped into bite-sized pieces

2 tbsp of coconut

½ tsp of pink Himalayan salt

½ tsp of black pepper, ground

Preparation:

Mix together vinegar, salt, and pepper in a mixing bowl. Set aside.

Combine the vegetables in a large bowl. Add apple slices and pine nuts. Toss well to combine and serve.

Nutritional information per serving: Calories: 85, Protein: 2.0g Carbs: 8.8g Fats: 5.6g

19. Brown Rice Pudding with Raspberries and Chia Seeds

Ingredients:

¾ cup of brown rice

1 cup of almond milk

¼ cup of honey

1 tbsp of coconut oil

¼ tsp of pink Himalayan salt

½ cup of raspberries

¼ cup of walnuts

2 tbsp of chia seeds

Preparation:

Bring 2 cups of water to a boil. Add rice and reduce the heat. Cover and cook for about 15 minutes.

Now add one cup of almond milk, honey, coconut oil, and salt. Continue to cook for five more minutes. Remove from the heat and cool for a while.

Top with fresh raspberries, walnuts, and chia seeds. Serve.

Nutrition information per serving: Kcal: 451, Protein: 8.6g, Carbs: 53.9g, Fats: 24.6g

20. Avocado Pineapple Salad

Ingredients:

1 cup of avocado chunks

1 cup of pineapple chunks

1 cup of watermelon

1 cup of sour cream

1 cup of spinach, finely chopped

1 tbsp of honey

1 tsp of vanilla extract

1 tbsp of flaxseeds

Preparation:

In a medium bowl, combine sour cream, honey, vanilla extract, and flaxseeds. Stir well to combine and set aside.

Wash and prepare the vegetables.

Peel the avocado and pineapple and cut in half. Remove the pit from the avocado and cut into small chunks along with pineapple. Place in a large salad bowl and set aside.

Cut one large watermelon wedge and peel it. Cut into bite-sized pieces and discard the seeds. Add it to the bowl with other fruits and set aside.

Wash the spinach thoroughly under cold running water and roughly chop it. Add it to the bowl with other fruits.

Now, pour the sour cream mixture over the fruits and veggies and toss well to coat all the ingredients.

Refrigerate for 15 minutes before serving.

Nutrition information per serving: Kcal: 346, Protein: 4.7g, Carbs: 25.5g, Fats: 26.5g

21. Green Delicious Apples with Broccoli

Ingredients

2 cups of broccoli, halved

2 large green delicious apples, roughly chopped

2 tbsp of olive oil

1 tbsp of dried parsley

½ tsp of pink Himalayan salt

3 cups of water

Preparation:

Bring the water to boil in a deep pot. Add broccoli and cook for about 20 minutes, or until soft. You can try this with a fork. Remove from the heat and drain. Allow it to cool for a while and cut each broccoli in half. Wash and roughly chop the apples. Combine it with broccoli in a bowl and season with olive oil and salad seasoning.

Nutrition information per serving: Kcal: 291 Protein: 4.2g, Carbs: 13.2g, Fats: 14.7g

22. Almond Milk and Spinach Smoothie

Ingredients:

2 cups of baby spinach, roughly chopped

1 cup of almond milk

½ avocado, roughly chopped

½ cup fresh mint leaves

1 cup of water

1 tbsp of honey

A handful of ice cubes

Preparation:

Combine the ingredients in a blender and pulse until smoot. Serve cold.

Nutrition information per serving: Kcal: 427 Protein: 5.3g, Carbs: 22.6g, Fats: 38.7g

23. Homemade Chicken Soup

Ingredients:

1 lb chicken meat

½ cup of soup noodles

4 cups of chicken broth

A handful of fresh parsley

1 tsp of salt

¼ tsp of freshly ground black pepper

Preparation:

For this recipe, I always try to find an organic chicken. They are much tastier and better for a homemade soup. Use both, dark and white pieces and rinse well under the running water. Pat dry with a kitchen paper and place on a clean work surface.

Using a sharp paring knife, cut chicken into bite-sized pieces. Sprinkle with salt and place in a deep pot. If using organic chicken, be careful not to add extra fat because this meat already has enough fat.

Pour in the chicken broth and cover with a lid. Cook for 45 minutes, over medium-high heat.

Now add soup noodles and reduce the heat to minimum. Cook for five more minutes.

Sprinkle with some freshly ground black pepper and parsley.

Serve warm.

Nutrition information per serving: Kcal: 282, Protein: 38.6g, Carbs: 6g, Dietary Fibers: 0g, Sugars: 0.6g, Fats: 10.2g, Saturated Fats: 2.8g

24. Swiss Chard Stew with Soft Chicken Meat

Ingredients:

2 lbs chicken meat, dark and white meat

2 lbs Swiss chard, chopped

2 cups of chicken broth

2 tbsp butter, unsalted

2 tbsp olive oil

1 tsp sea salt

Preparation:

Thoroughly rinse the meat and pat dry with a kitchen paper. Using a sharp paring knife, cut the meat into smaller pieces.

Rinse well the Swiss chard. Always look for organic vegetables. They can be a bit messier to clean but are definitely worth it. Chop and drain in a colander.

Place the meat in a large, heavy-bottomed pot. Add two cups of chicken broth, season with salt, and bring it to a boil. Cook until fork-tender. Remove from the heat and drain. Reserve the liquid for some other recipe.

In the same pot, melt the butter over medium-high heat. Add Swiss chard and stir-fry for five minutes. Season with salt, pepper, or some turmeric. Serve with chicken.

Nutrition information per serving: Kcal: 484, Protein: 57.8g, Carbs: 7.2g, Dietary Fibers: 3g, Sugars: 2.3g, Fats: 24.7g, Saturated Fats: 7.6g

25. Kidney Bean Stew

Ingredients:

7 oz red beans, pre-cooked

2 medium-sized carrots, chopped

2 celery stalks

1 large onion, peeled and finely chopped

2 tbsp of tomato paste

1 tbsp of all-purpose flour

½ tbsp of cayenne pepper

1 bay leaf

1 cup of vegetable broth

3 tbsp of extra virgin olive oil

1 tsp of salt

A handful of fresh parsley

Preparation:

Rinse well the celery stalks and cut into about half-inch thick pieces. Set aside.

Peel the carrots to remove the outer layers. Using a sharp paring knife, finely chop each carrot into small pieces.

Heat up the olive oil in a medium-sized skillet and add onions. Sautee until translucent. Add celery stalks and chopped carrots. Continue to cook for five more minutes, adding one tablespoon of vegetable broth at the time.

Now add red beans, cayenne pepper, bay leaf, salt, parsley, and tomato paste. Stir in one tablespoon of all-purpose flour and pour in the remaining vegetable broth.

Cook for 25 minutes, over medium-high heat, stirring constantly.

Sprinkle with some fresh parsley and serve warm.

Nutrition information per serving: Kcal: 311, Protein: 13.7g, Carbs: 40.8g, Dietary Fibers: 9.8g, Sugars: 5.5g, Fats: 11.6g, Saturated Fats: 1.7g

26. Lean Shrimp Stew with Brussels Sprouts

Ingredients:

1 lb of large shrimps, cleaned

7 oz of Brussels sprouts, outer leaves removed

5 oz of okra, whole

2 small carrots, sliced

3 oz of baby corn

2 cups of chicken broth

2 large tomatoes, diced

2 tbsp of tomato paste

½ tsp of chili pepper, ground

¼ tsp of black pepper, freshly ground

1 tsp of sea salt

1 cup of olive oil

¼ cup of balsamic vinegar

1 tbsp of fresh rosemary, finely chopped

1 small celery stalk, for decoration

2 tbsp of sour cream, optionally

Preparation:

Wash the shrimps under cold running water and drain in a large colander. Set aside.

Combine olive oil, balsamic vinegar, rosemary, salt, and pepper in a large bowl. Stir well and place the shrimps into the bowl. Toss well to coat and refrigerate for 20 minutes to allow flavors to meld into the shrimps.

Meanwhile, wash and prepare the vegetables. Trim off the outer layers of the Brussels sprouts and slice the carrots.

First, place diced tomatoes a deep pot, along with tomato paste, 2 tablespoons of olive oil, and chili pepper. Cook for 15 minutes, over medium-high heat, stirring constantly. Remove the sauce to a medium-sized bowl and cover with a lid. Set aside.

Now, pour the chicken broth into your pot and add Brussels sprouts, carrots, and okra. Sprinkle with some salt, pepper, and cover. Simmer for 20 minutes, stirring occasionally.

When the vegetables are fork-tender, remove them from the pot. Set aside.

Place the shrimps in the remaining broth and bring it to a boil. Add some water if necessary and cook for 7 minutes. Drain and set aside.

Preheat the remaining oil in a large saucepan over a medium-high heat. Add previously cooked vegetables and add baby corn. Stir well and cook for about 2-3 minutes. Remove from the heat and transfer to a serving bowl. Add shrimps and tomato sauce.

Nutrition information per serving: Kcal: 193, Protein: 15.7g, Carbs: 20g, Dietary Fibers: 4.3g, Sugars: 5.2g, Fats: 7.2g, Saturated Fats: 1.4g

27. Leek Omelet

Ingredients:

1 lb fresh leek, chopped into bite-sized pieces

7-8 garlic cloves, whole

1 tbsp butter, unsalted

2 tbsp olive oil

4 large eggs

1 tsp salt

Preparation:

In a large skillet, heat up the olive oil and add chopped leek and whole garlic cloves. Stir-fry for ten minutes, stirring constantly. Stir in one tablespoon of butter and add eggs but make sure to keep them whole. This recipe requires poached eggs. Cook for 3 more minutes, and remove from the heat. Serve immediately.

Nutrition information per serving: Kcal: 468, Protein: 16.7g, Carbs: 36.3g, Dietary Fibers: 4.3g, Sugars: 9.7g, Fats: 30.4g, Saturated Fats: 8.8g

28. Spring Spinach Smoothie

Ingredients:

¼ cup of spinach, finely chopped

¼ cup of broccoli, finely chopped

1 tbsp of walnuts, minced

1 tbsp of hazelnuts, minced

2 cups of water

¼ tsp of ginger, ground

A handful of ice cubes

Preparation:

Combine spinach and broccoli in a colander and wash under cold running water. Drain and place in a blender along with all other ingredients. Pulse for 30 seconds and then transfer to a serving glass.

Add some ice and serve immediately.

Nutrition information per serving: Kcal: 44, Protein: 1.7g, Carbs: 1.8g, Fats: 3.8g

29. Lentil Burger Wraps

Ingredients:

1 cup lentils, pre-cooked

1 oz spinach, finely chopped

¼ cup feta cheese

1 tsp fresh rosemary, finely chopped

¼ cup bread crumbs

5 tbsp olive oil

1 onion, peeled and sliced

3 tbsp sweet corn

A handful of fresh lettuce, finely chopped

5-6 cherry tomatoes

5 whole grain wraps

Preparation:

In a large bowl, combine lentils with spinach, feta, rosemary, bread crumbs, and three tablespoons of olive oil. Shape bite-sized balls and gently flatten them in the middle. Set aside.

Heat up the remaining oil in a large skillet. Gently place burgers in the skillet and cook for 2-3 minutes on each side, or until light brown.

Meanwhile, sprinkle some water on each wrap and microwave for one minute. Set aside.

Divide burgers between five wraps. Add some lettuce, onions, corn, and cherry tomatoes to each wrap. Fold over and secure with some toothpicks.

Serve immediately.

Nutrition information per serving: Kcal: 496, Protein: 17.6g, Carbs: 66.6g, Dietary Fibers: 16.1g, Sugars: 5.7g, Fats: 19.5g, Saturated Fats: 3.4g

30. Lentil Spread

Ingredients:

1 lb of lentils, pre-cooked

1 cup of sweet corn

3 large tomatoes, diced

3 tbsp of tomato paste

½ tsp of dried oregano, ground

2 tbsp of Parmesan cheese

1 tsp of salt

½ tsp of red pepper flakes

3 tbsp of olive oil

¼ cup of vegetable broth

Preparation:

Heat up some olive oil in a medium-sized pot. Add diced tomatoes, tomato paste, and ½ cup of water. Sprinkle with some oregano and bring it to a boil. Cook for five minutes, stirring constantly.

Now add lentils, sweet corn, and broth. Bring it to a boil

and simmer over medium heat for 15 minutes.

Remove from the heat and cool completely. Transfer to the refrigerator and chill for at least 30 minutes before serving.

Top with grated Parmesan and enjoy.

Nutrition information per serving: Kcal: 297, Protein: 17.3g, Carbs: 41.9g, Dietary Fibers: 19g, Sugars: 4.4g, Fats: 7g, Saturated Fats: 1.4g

31. Brown Rice with Stewed Vegetables

Ingredients:

1 cup of brown rice, uncooked

8oz fresh cauliflower

2 medium-sized carrots, sliced

1 medium sized cellery root, sliced

1 tsp of pink Himalayan salt

½ tsp of freshly ground black pepper

2 tbsp of extra coconut oil

1 tablespoon of fresh celery, finely chopped

Preparation:

Place one cup of brown rice in a deep pot. Add three cups of water and bring it to a boil. Reduce the heat and continue to cook until the liquid evaporates. Remove from the heat and set aside.

Meanwhile, boil the vegetables and cook until soft. Remove from the heat and drain.

Melt the coconut oil over a medium-hogh heat. Add cooked rice, salt, pepper and stir-fry for 3-4 minutes. Mix well and serve with sliced vegetables.

Add some chopped celery and serve warm.

Nutrition information per serving: Kcal: 399 Protein: 10g, Carbs: 84.8g, Fats: 2.7g

32. Lean Broccoli Stew with Thyme

Ingredients:

2 oz fresh broccoli

A handful of fresh parsley, finely chopped

1 tsp of dried thyme, ground

1 tbsp of freshly squeezed lemon juice

3 tbsp of coconut oil

1 tbsp of cashew cream

Preparation:

Place the broccoli in a deep pot and pour enough water to cover. Bring it to a boil and cook until tender. Remove from the heat and drain.

Transfer to a food processor. Add fresh parsley, thyme, and about ½ cup of water. Pulse until smooth mixture. Return to a pot and add some more water. Bring it to a boil and cook for several minutes, over a minimum temperature.

Stir in some coconut oil and cashew cream, sprinkle with fresh lemon juice. Serve warm.

Nutrition information per serving: Kcal: 377 Protein: 1.8g, Carbs: 4.7g, Fats: 41.2g

33. Marinated Smelt Risotto

Ingredients:

1 lb fresh smelts, cleaned and heads removed

1 cup extra virgin olive oil

½ cup freshly squeezed lemon juice

¼ cup freshly squeezed orange juice

1 tbsp Dijon mustard

1 tsp fresh rosemary, finely chopped

2 garlic cloves, crushed

1 tsp sea salt

½ cup of rice

7 oz okra

1 large carrot, sliced

¼ cup green peas, soaked overnight

7 oz cherry tomatoes, halved

4 tbsp vegetable oil

2 cups fish stock

Preparation:

In a large bowl, combine olive oil with lemon juice, orange juice, dijon, garlic, salt, and rosemary. Stir well and submerge fish in this mixture. Refrigerate for one hour.

Meanwhile, grease the bottom of a medium-sized pot with vegetable poil. Add sliced carrots, peas, cherry tomatoes, and okra. Simmer for ten minuts, stirring constantly.

Now add rice and fish stock. Bring it to a boil and cook for ten minutes over medium-high heat.

Remove the fish from the refrigerator and add to the pot along with half of the marinade. Continue to cook for 5 more minutes.

Nutrition information per serving: Kcal: 583, Protein: 30.1g, Carbs: 24.7g, Dietary Fibers: 3.2g, Sugars: 4.4g, Fats: 40.7g, Saturated Fats: 6.8g

34. Citrus Catfish Fillets

Ingredients:

1 lb catfish fillets

1 cup of olive oil

½ lemon, sliced

¼ cup of lemon juice, freshly squeezed

1 tsp of dry rosemary, ground

1 tbsp of fresh parsley, finely chopped

3 garlic cloves, crushed

¼ tsp of pink Himalayan salt

Preparation:

Rinse the fillets under cold running water and pat dry with a kitchen paper.

Combine the olive oil, lemon juice, rosemary, parsley, garlic, and salt in a bowl and stir well. Submerge the fillets in this mixture and refrigerate for 30 minutes (it can stand in the refrigerator up to 2 hours).

Meanwhile, preheat the oven to 300 degrees. Line some parchment paper over a baking sheet and set aside.

Remove the fish from the refrigerator and transfer to a baking sheet. Add half of the marinade and cook for about 30 minutes.

Remove from the oven, sprinkle with some more marinade and serve with lemon slices and some vegetables of your choice.

Nutrition information per serving: Kcal: 421, Protein: 27g, Carbs: 2.6g, Fats: 34g

35. Roasted Pecans and Arugula Salad

Ingredients:

1 lb of fresh arugula, chopped

1 large apple, pitted and wedged

2 tbsp of lemon juice, freshly squeezed

1 small onion, sliced

2 tbsp of extra-virgin olive oil

2 oz of pecans, roughly chopped

1 tbsp of liquid honey

1 tsp of pink Himalayan salt

¼ tsp of black pepper, freshly ground

Preparation:

Preheat the oven to 300°F.

Line some parchment paper over a baking sheet and spread nuts over it. Place it in the oven and bake for 10 minutes, or until golden brown. Remove from the oven and set aside to cool for a while.

In a small bowl, combine lemon juice, oil, honey, salt, and

pepper. Stir until well incorporated and set aside to allow flavors to meld.

Wash the arugula thoroughly under cold running water. Drain and roughly chop it in a large salad bowl. Set aside.

Wash the apple and cut in half. Remove the core and slice the apple into wedges. Add it to the bowl with arugula and set aside.

Peel the onion and slice into thin slices. Add it to the bowl with other ingredients.

Now, drizzle the salad with dressing and toss well until coat all the ingredients. Top with roasted pecans and serve immediately.

Nutrition information per serving: Kcal: 241, Protein: 4.9g, Carbs: 20.1g, Fats: 18g

36. Rice Rolls

Ingredients:

40 wine leaves, fresh

1 cup of brown rice

2 tbsp olive oil

3 garlic cloves, crushed

¼ cup of lemon juice, freshly squeezed

2 tbsp fresh mint

½ tsp of pink Himalayan salt

Preparation:

Wash the leaves thoroughly, one at a time. Place on a clean working surface. Grease the bottom of a deep pot with oil and make a layer with wine leaves. Set aside.

In a medium-sized bowl, combine rice with oil, garlic, mint, salt, and pepper. Place one wine leaf at a time on a working surface and add one teaspoon of filling at the bottom end. Fold the leaf over the filling towards the center. Bring the two sides in towards the center and roll them up tightly. Gently transfer to a pot.

Add 2 cups of water and lemon juice. Cover and cook for 30 minutes, over medium-high heat.

Remove from the pot and chill overnight in the refrigerator.

Nutrition information per serving: Kcal: 313, Protein: 2.9g, Carbs: 30.4, Fats: 20.5g

37. Asian Asparagus Salad

Ingredients:

1 lb of wild asparagus, trimmed

1 cup of spring onions, chopped

1 cup of red cabbage, chopped

1 tbsp of white wine vinegar

1 tbsp of olive oil

½ tsp of ginger, freshly grated

½ tsp of pink Himalayan salt

¼ tsp of black pepper, ground

Preparation:

Place the asparagus in a pot of boiling water. Cook for about 3-5 minutes, or until soften. Remove from the heat and soak in cold water for a while.

Meanwhile, combine canola oil, ginger, vinegar, chili, salt, and pepper in a mixing bowl.

Drain well the asparagus and place in a large bowl and add spring onions and red cabbage. Drizzle with dressing and toss all well to coat. Serve immediately.

Nutrition information per serving: Kcal: 91, Protein: 4.3g, Carbs: 10.2g, Fats: 5.0g

38. Citrus Quinoa Porridge

Ingredients:

1 cup of white quinoa

2 tbsp of lemon juice, freshly squeezed

¼ tsp of pink Himalayan salt

1 tsp of lemon zest, freshly grated

2 cups of vegetable stock, unsalted

1 tbsp of coconut oil

Preparation:

Combine quinoa and water in a medium pot. Bring it to a boil and then reduce the heat to low. Add lemon juice and butter. Sprinkle with lemon zest and a pinch of salt. Cover with a lid and cook for another 15 minutes. Remove from the heat and serve.

Nutrition information per serving: Kcal: 132, Protein: 3.7g, Carbs: 18.1g, Fats: 6.8g

39. Red Pollock Stew

Ingredients:

1 lb pollock fillet

4 garlic cloves, crushed

4 large tomatoes, peeled

2 bay leaves, whole

2 cups fish stock

1 teaspoon freshly ground black pepper

1 large onion, peeled and finely chopped

½ cup extra virgin olive oil

1 teaspoon sea salt

Preparation:

In a large skillet, heat up two tablespoons of olive oil. Add finely chopped onion and cook until translucent, stirring constantly. Add tomatoes and continue to cook until completely soft, adding some fish stock from time to time.

When tomatoes have softened and the liquid has evaporated, add the remaining ingredients and one cup of water. Bring it to a boil and cook for 15 minutes.

Nutrition information per serving: Kcal: 404, Protein: 28.1g, Carbs: 9.5g, Dietary Fibers: 2.6g, Sugars: 5.1g, Fats: 28.9g, Saturated Fats: 4.5g

40. Sesame Seed Risotto with Lamb

Ingredients:

1 cup of rice

1 cup of green peas

14 oz of lamb, tender cuts

3 tbsp of sesame seeds

3 cups of beef broth

1 tsp of sea salt

1 bay leaf

½ tsp of dried thyme

3 tbsp of butter

Preparation:

Wash the meat and place on a clean working surface. Slice into approximately 1/2-inch thick slices. Place in the pressure cooker and add beef broth. Close the lid and set the steam release handle. Cook for about 20 minutes, depending on thype of your cooker. Release the steam and remove the meat, but reserve the liquid. The meat should be fork-tender.

Transfer to a deep pot. Add rice, green peas, and the remaining broth. Bring it to a boil and reduce the heat to minimum. Simmer for 10 more minutes, stirring occasionally.

Remove from the heat and stir in three tablespoons of butter and sesame seeds.

Serve immediately.

Nutrition information per serving: Kcal: 498, Protein: 34.4g, Carbs: 43.9g, Dietary Fibers: 3.3g, Sugars: 2.1g, Fats: 19.7g, Saturated Fats: 8.6g

41. Spinach and Lamb Soup

Ingredients:

1 lb lamb rack

7 oz spinach, torn

2 medium-sized onions, finely chopped

3 tbsp olive oil

4 cups beef broth

½ tsp sea salt

½ tsp Italian seasoning mix

Preparation:

Rinse well the meat and rub with sea salt and Italian seasoning mix. Place in a deep pot and add broth. Bring it to a boil and cook for 45 minutes.

Remove from the heat and set aside.

Grease the bottom of a large skillet with olive oil. Add onions and stir-fry for 5 minutes. Now add spinach and continue to cook for 5 more minutes.

Finally, add meat, broth, and one more cup of water. Bring it to a boil and remove from the heat.

Serve immediately.

Nutrition information per serving: Kcal: 373, Protein: 38.7g, Carbs: 7.8g, Dietary Fibers: 2.3g, Sugars: 3.2g, Fats: 20.4g, Saturated Fats: 4.9g

42. Beet Apple and Spinach Salad

Ingredients:

1 large beet, steamed and sliced

2 cups of spinach, trimmed

2 spring onions, finely chopped

1 small green apple

¼ cup of olive oil

2 tbsp of fresh lime juice

1 tbsp of honey

1 garlic clove, crushed

1 tsp of apple cider

¼ tsp of freshly ground black pepper

¼ tsp of pink Himalayan salt

Preparation:

Place the beet in a deep pot. Pour enough water to cover and cook for about 40 minutes, or until tender. Remove the skin and slice. Transfer to a bowl. Combine olive oil, vinegar, cider, salt, pepper, and honey. Pour over beet slices and toss to coat. Let it stand for at least 30 minutes.

Wash and pat dry the apple. Slice into thin strips and combine with beet slices, spring onions, and spinach. Add crushed garlic and mix well. Serve.

Nutrition information per serving: Kcal: 365 Protein: 3.3g, Carbs: 37.1g, Fats: 25.8g

43.   Beet Greens and Kale with Garlic Dressing

Ingredients:

1 cup of beet greens, rinsed and chopped

2 cups of kale, rinsed and chopped

2 spring onions, finely chopped

For dressing:

2 garlic cloves, crushed

3 tbsp of cilantro, finely chopped

1 orange

¼ cup of raw cashews

¼ cup of olive oil

A pinch of pink Himalayan salt

Preparation:

Combine the dressing ingredients in a food processor and mix well until creamy mixture. Set aside.

Place the beet greens in a sauce pan and pour enough water to cover. Bring it to a boil and cook for a couple of minutes. Remove from the heat and drain. Cool for a while and transfer to a bowl. Add chopped kale and spring onion, pour the dressing over the salad and toss well to combine.

Nutrition information per serving: Kcal: 407 Protein: 6.8g, Carbs: 26.6g, Fats: 33.4g

44. Thick Fish Soup with Peas

Ingredients:

7 oz mackerel fillets

½ cup wheat groats, soaked

½ cup kidney beans, soaked

¼ cup sweet corn

1 lb fresh tomatoes, peeled and roughly chopped

4 cups fish stock

4 tbsp extra virgin olive oil

1 tsp sea salt

1 tsp fresh rosemary, finely chopped

3 garlic cloves, crushed

Preparation:

Grease the botton of a deep pot with olive oil. Add crushed garlic and tomatoes and cook for 5 minutes over medium heat.

Now add rosemary, fish stock, salt, corn, kidney beans, and wheat groats. Cover and reduce the heat to minimum.

Simmer for 20 minutes.

Finally, add mackerel fillets and cook for 10 more minutes.

Serve immediately.

Nutrition information per serving: Kcal: 479, Protein: 26.8g, Carbs: 38.3g, Dietary Fibers: 8.2g, Sugars: 3.9g, Fats: 25.7g, Saturated Fats: 4.7g

45. Thick Lentil Soup

Ingredients:

1 cup of brown lentils

1 large onion, peeled and finely chopped

2 large carrots, sliced

1 large sweet potato, peeled and chopped

2 large celery stalks, sliced

3 tbsp of extra virgin olive oil

3 large garlic cloves, minced

4 cups of beef broth

1 tsp of thyme, dried

1 tsp of salt

¼ tsp of freshly ground black pepper

Preparation:

In a medium-sized pot, heat up the oil and add onions, garlic, and sliced celery. Cook for 5 minutes, stirring constantly.

Now add lentils, sliced carrot, and chopped potato. Stir in

salt, pepper, and thyme. Pour in the broth and stir well.

Cover with the lid and bring it to a boil. Reduce the heat to minimum and simmer for 20 minutes.

Remove from the heat and serve immediately.

Nutrition information per serving: Kcal: 541, Protein: 30.8g, Carbs: 44.3g, Dietary Fibers: 14.9g, Sugars: 4.7g, Fats: 26.7g, Saturated Fats: 7g

46. Egg Salad

Ingredients:

3 eggs, boiled

1 yellow bell pepper, sliced and seeds removed

1 red onion, sliced

1 medium-sized tomato, roughly chopped

1 small cucumber, sliced

a handful of lettuce, torn

7 oz fresh goat's cheese

1 tsp sea salt

4 tbsp extra virgin olive oil

1 tbsp freshly squeezed lemon juice

Preparation:

Boil a medium-sized pot of water. Gently place the eggs in it and cook for 10 minutes. Remove from the heat and drain. Cool for a while.

Meanwhile, combine vegetables in a large bowl. Peel and slice eggs. Transfer to a bowl. Add fresh goat's cheese and season with salt.

Drizzle with olive oil and freshly squeezed lemon juice. Serve immediately.

Nutrition information per serving: Kcal: 389, Protein: 16.4g, Carbs: 11.1g, Fats: 32.4g

ADDITIONAL TITLES FROM THIS AUTHOR

70 Effective Meal Recipes to Prevent and Solve Being Overweight: Burn Fat Fast by Using Proper Dieting and Smart Nutrition

By Joe Correa CSN

48 Acne Solving Meal Recipes: The Fast and Natural Path to Fixing Your Acne Problems in Less Than 10 Days!

By Joe Correa CSN

41 Alzheimer's Preventing Meal Recipes: Reduce or Eliminate Your Alzheimer's Condition in 30 Days or Less!

By Joe Correa CSN

70 Effective Breast Cancer Meal Recipes: Prevent and Fight Breast Cancer with Smart Nutrition and Powerful Foods

By Joe Correa CSN